THE GHOSTLY TALES OF AUSTIN

Published by Arcadia Children's Books
A Division of Arcadia Publishing
Charleston, SC
www.arcadiapublishing.com

Spooky America is a trademark of Arcadia Publishing, Inc.

First published 2021

Manufactured in the United States

ISBN 978-1-4671-9820-2

Library of Congress Control Number: 2021938346

Notice: The information in this book is true and complete to the best of our knowledge. It is offered without guarantee on the part of the author or Arcadia Publishing. The author and Arcadia Publishing disclaim all liability in connection with the use of this book.

All images courtesy of Shutterstock.com; p.72 Ritu Manoj Jethani/Shutterstock.com; p.94 Rob Crandall/Shutterstock.com

THE
GHOSTLY TALES
OF
AUSTIN

CARIE JUETTNER

Adapted from *Haunted Austin* by Jeanine Plumer

arcadia®
CHILDREN'S BOOKS

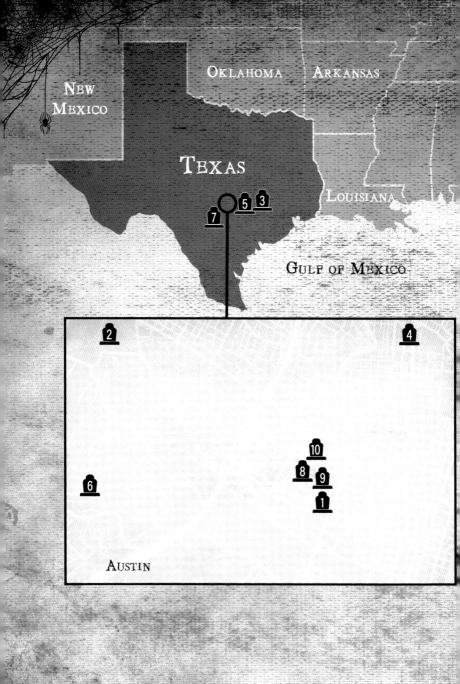

TABLE OF CONTENTS & MAP KEY

Introduction 3

Chapter 1. A Flood of Tragedy. 9

1 Moonshine Grill

2 Great Granite Dam

Chapter 2. Hope from Beyond the Grave 21

3 Hornsby Bend

Chapter 3. Old Souls 33

4 3710 Cedar Street

5 Chapter 4. The Mysteries of Mount Bonnell 45

Chapter 5. The Ghost Wagon of Westlake 53

6 Eanes Creek

7 Chapter 6. Swen Beryman: Settler, Store Owner…Specter? 61

8 Chapter 7. The Driskill Hotel. 73

Chapter 8. Unusual Undertakings 85

9 Hannig Building

10 Chapter 9. The Governing Ghosts of the Texas Capitol. 95

Chapter 10. Last Words 107

Introduction

Texas has a big personality, and no city embodies its soul more than its capital, Austin. Set deep in the heart of Texas on the banks of the Colorado River, Austin is known for its live music, rich history, and lush hiking and bike trails. Through the years, it has become a popular place to visit, and many people enjoy their time here so much they decide to stay. That's why this Central Texas town was named the sixth fastest-growing city in America in 2020.

A person with a day to spend in Austin might start with a visit to the Bullock Texas State History Museum, followed by a stroll through the beautiful grounds of the University of Texas—home of the Longhorns—which is just across the street. Then, after a taco or some mouthwatering Texas barbecue, they might walk the trails of the Lady Bird Johnson Wildflower Center in southwest Austin or get some sun in Zilker Park, where the popular Austin City Limits Music Festival is held each year. After that it will be time for a dip in Barton Springs, the natural pool that's sixty-eight degrees year-round (and much appreciated during the oppressive heat of Austin summers).

When the sun goes down, the nightlife begins. A guest can catch a concert at Stubb's or visit the shops and restaurants along Congress Avenue. One of the most unique sights to see in Austin is beneath the Congress Avenue Bridge, which houses the largest urban bat colony in North America. Yep, *bats*. One and a half million Mexican free-tailed bats

call the bridge home, and every year from late spring to early fall, people come from all over to watch the colony emerge from its roosting place at dusk and sweep across the sky in a giant cloud. It's a sight you'll never forget.

But Austin is not just about guitars, good food, and fun. There are more than a few creepy characters you must watch out for in the city, and we don't just mean the rattlesnakes. Amidst the live oaks and limestone, restless spirits walk. Ghosts of murdered men and victims of tragic natural disasters lurk in some

of the city's most famous streets and sites. Even the capitol building is haunted! So if you decide to visit, keep your eyes peeled for strangers who are *extra* strange.

After all, the city's motto is "Keep Austin Weird," and the ghosts are definitely doing their part.

A Flood of Tragedy

Nature can be scary. Hurricanes sink ships, tornados rip roofs off houses, and earthquakes topple buildings. These disasters and the memories they create can cause nightmares. In fact, one of the most haunting things ever to happen to the city of Austin started out with just a little rain.

In 1900, the part of the Colorado River that's known today as Lake Austin was called

Lake McDonald, and this popular recreation spot was formed by the Great Granite Dam. The dam had been completed in 1893, and it was something Austinites were proud of. The massive structure was longer than three football fields, and it was four stories high and just as thick. It was so famous it was even featured on the cover of *Scientific American* magazine.

However, the dam had a problem. Three years after construction, the Austin mayor received a letter from the dam's former chief construction engineer, Joseph Frizell. Frizell had been forced to leave his job before the dam was finished, but now he wrote to warn the mayor of a problem on the dam's east side. The following year, a fisherman noticed a hole beneath the dam that was six feet long. And in 1899, a leak on the east side of the dam was patched with clay. But no one took these discoveries seriously. The Great Granite Dam was a marvel of human engineering. They decided not to worry about a few small imperfections. But they should have, because what happened next changed Austin forever.

On April 6, 1900, it started to rain. At first, it was just a normal spring rainstorm, but it soon turned into something much worse. The water kept falling harder and harder. By the morning of Saturday, April 7, when the storm finally dried to a light drizzle, seventeen inches of rain had dropped on the town, and the water had risen eleven feet above the top of the dam. It poured over in a great, turbulent waterfall. The sight was so remarkable that people flocked to see it. No one saw any harm in visiting the mighty structure. After all, the rain had stopped. What could go wrong?

By mid-morning, hundreds of people stood on the banks of the Colorado

River, watching the awesome sight. They were still standing there at 11:15 a.m. when a deep boom emanated from the concrete structure. The dam split down the middle, and the east side collapsed.

The dam's job was to hold back Lake McDonald, a thirty-mile long, one-mile-wide body of water. When the dam crumbled, the lake came through. A fifty-foot wall of water rushed downstream into an already flooded river, swallowing everything in its path.

Several dozen people lost their lives in the 1900 flood. Many of those who came to see the gushing dam were swept away, as were the families who lived on the banks of the river. But countless tragedies occurred downstream, as well. The river rose seventeen inches *an hour* until 3:00 that afternoon. Nearby Shoal Creek and Waller Creek rose twenty feet in just two hours. The impact of the water was devastating.

The bodies of humans and animals, as well as farm equipment and even buildings, were all caught in the vicious torrent and washed away, never to be seen again.

Onlookers saw one man running for his life from the advancing flood waters. At the last minute, he reached a telephone pole and hoisted himself to safety. The people watching cheered in relief, but the man's good luck soon ran out. A house that was caught in the surging river struck the telephone pole, and the man lost his grip while onlookers watched helplessly.

At the hydroelectric plant just downstream from the dam was an even more ghastly scene. Nine people, three of them just young boys, were working in the lowest level of the powerhouse when the dam broke and water started pouring in. Only one man survived. He threw his belt over a piece of metal above him and pulled himself above the water, where he could breathe. The other eight drowned. Their bodies remained trapped for more than a day until the water receded and a hole was blasted in the wall, finally allowing the corpses to escape.

Amidst the scenes of heartbreak and horror, heroes could be found as well. Henry Robell was one of the people who went to visit Lake McDonald on the fateful morning of April 7, 1900, but when the dam started to collapse, he leaped into action. When Henry saw the first signs that the structure was crumbling, he jumped on his horse and raced along the northern bank of the river into the city. As his horse galloped ahead of the raging waters, Henry shouted, "The dam has [broken]! Run to high ground!" It's unclear how many people

Henry Robell rescued with his warning, but it's certain his quick thinking saved lives.

Unfortunately, the peril didn't end when the waters receded. In the wake of the flood, Austinites had to deal with new concerns, such as homelessness, disease, and fire danger. Those who could opened their homes to neighbors, and nearby cities sent supplies and extra fire trucks to the suffering town.

Piece by piece, Austin put itself back together. The victims were buried, and houses and buildings were repaired or rebuilt. The sun returned to Central Texas and shone down on a city of resilient people determined to move forward from the catastrophe.

But the great storm and the tragedy sown in its wake would never be forgotten. People often visited the former dam to look at the rubble left behind and to remember the good times they'd had at Lake McDonald, which was now gone.

Now, where you find tragedy, you often find ghosts, and many people lost their lives in the 1900 flood, meeting their untimely end. But some say that spirits still linger. After the flood, rumors began circulating about mysterious lights shining beneath the water at the site of the collapsed dam. The gossip gained momentum as more and more people saw the eerie glow. The lights came from under the water. They were round and clear and moved around near the surface before disappearing again.

Searching for the lights became a popular hobby of teenagers. On summer nights, they would visit what is now Red Bud Isle. Sometimes they brought fishing poles, but it wasn't really fish they were interested in. They wanted to see the lights, and sometimes they did. But what were these ghostly orbs floating up from the depths of the river? No one knows for sure, but many people believe they were the spirits of those lost to the 1900 flood.

One of the structures that survived the Austin flood was the sturdily built Hofheintz-Reissig building, at the corner of Third Street and Red River. When most of the neighboring houses washed away, this stone structure remained, and its owners did what they could to care for those suffering nearby.

Today, the Hofheintz-Reissig home is the site of the Moonshine Bar & Grill, where Austin serves up some of the most delicious chicken and waffles you can find. Stop in for brunch and sink your teeth into a piece of crispy, golden chicken followed by a bite of buttery waffle dipped in maple syrup. While you are enjoying your food, if you hear a crash in the kitchen, it's likely that someone has dropped something. Most of the time, anyway. Strange things can occur at the Moonshine Grill.

Mason jars have been known to shatter while sitting at the restaurant's empty tables, and glassware sometimes flies off the shelves for no reason. A pitcher of water seated securely on a rubber mat once flew four feet into the air before plunging to the floor, creating a terrible mess as well as a fright. The owner of the restaurant once saw the tray of the office printer launch itself at him after he attempted—without success—to print something. Other times, staff members have heard the sound of breaking glass without ever finding evidence of any.

An Austin tour guide named Monica once stopped into Moonshine on a cold February night only to be greeted by a mist that formed near the hostess stand. The misty figure drifted past Monica, touching the side of her face as it slid by, sending a shiver down her side. The mist moved down the hall toward the cellar stairs, then disappeared.

Some believe ghosts of flood victims are to blame for the chaos and creepiness at this popular Austin restaurant. Waller Creek flows just east of Moonshine, and in 1900, it carried away the bodies of nearby residents unable to escape the waters. It makes sense that the spirits of these lost souls would be drawn to the life and energy of the only remaining building from their time on Earth. Maybe they're just looking for a little warmth ... and some chicken and waffles.

CHAPTER 2

Hope from Beyond the Grave

Consider yourself warned: the tale you are about to read is chilling and gruesome and not for the faint of heart!

Several Native American tribes were present in Central Texas when Austin was founded, including the Tonkawa and Apache, but the most skilled warriors were the Comanche. The Comanche began moving south from Wyoming in the 1600s and had settled in Texas by the 1830s. The members of the tribe were accomplished riders, and their young men were trained from an early age to be warriors. Unfortunately, some of the encounters between European settlers and Comanche tribes resulted in violence.

In 1833, Josiah Wilbarger and Reuben Hornsby owned homesteads east of Austin, farthest from the heart of the city. Reuben's property, known as Hornsby's Bend, was especially beautiful and the envy of many. In the summer of that year, several new arrivals to Austin were camping on Hornsby's property. Their names were Mr. Haynie and Mr. Standifer, who had just arrived from Missouri, and Mr. Christian and Mr. Strother, who had recently settled in Austin.

In August, Wilbarger and the four campers boldly rode out into the frontier, following Walnut Creek straight into Comanche territory.

It wasn't long before the men rounded a bend and saw a lone Comanche warrior. Comanche were known to be fearsome, but there was only one of him and five of them, and some of these men harbored bitter feelings from past encounters with the tribe. Fueled by their anger and encouraged by the safety in numbers, the group chased the young Comanche, cutting him off and surrounding him with their horses. They taunted him, poked at him with their rifles, and dared him to fight before letting him go.

This was a very bad idea. The young warrior was not as alone as he had appeared. In fact, he was a scout for a war party that was only an hour's ride away.

Wilbarger and his group stopped for lunch near Pecan Springs. Wilbarger, Christian, and Strother unsaddled their horses and hobbled them, meaning they put restraints on their legs so they couldn't run away. Haynie and Standifer, who were new to Texas and nervous about their recent confrontation with the young Comanche, kept their horses saddled.

This decision saved their lives.

When the men were resting beneath the trees, war cries pierced the air, quickly followed by arrows and bullets as the Comanche war party attacked. The men scrambled for cover and tried to return fire, but some were not quick enough. Strother was the first to fall. Then Christian took a musket ball to the thigh, shattering his femur. Wilbarger pulled him behind a tree, but it was too late for Christian, who died from his wounds.

Wilbarger had been injured too; he had an arrow in his calf and a wound on his side. He saw Haynie and Standifer mount and begin riding away. Wilbarger cried out for them to stop, calling, "Take me with you!" When Haynie and Standifer heard their friend scream, they turned, considering the risk of going back for him. But right at that moment, Wilbarger was shot through the neck. He collapsed on the ground, and the attackers surrounded him. Assuming their companion was unable to be saved, Haynie and Standifer galloped away to safety.

However, Josiah Wilbarger wasn't dead. The bullet through his neck had not killed him. It had temporarily paralyzed him. He lay on the ground—unmoving and unblinking but alive— while the Comanche warriors robbed and scalped the victims around him. When it was Wilbarger's turn, he lay there while the men stole his clothing and then carved off a piece of his scalp. Comanches did not take the whole scalp, only a portion, about the size of a silver dollar. Wilbarger later said that his paralysis kept him from feeling the blade slice his skull, but the sound of the skin being ripped off his head was like distant thunder in his ears. The Comanche finished collecting their rewards and rode away, leaving Wilbarger unconscious in the afternoon sun wearing only one sock.

When Wilbarger woke, he was feverish, his whole body was aching, and he was intensely thirsty. He crawled to Walnut Creek and lay in the water for an hour, soothing his many painful wounds. Then he slept until the sun set. When he woke after dark, he tried to regain his strength by eating acorns and snails along the shore of the creek. His plan was to stay alive until someone found him. Then he made a grim discovery: there were maggots in his wounds.

Wilbarger realized he needed to get treatment as quickly as possible and resolved to crawl all the way back to Hornsby's Bend. But the ranch was six miles away. That's twenty-four laps around a track. In his weakened and wounded state, Wilbarger made it less than half a mile before he collapsed from exhaustion. He leaned against an oak tree, closed his eyes, and accepted that the end was near.

The next time Wilbarger opened his eyes, his sister, Margaret Clifton, was standing in front of him. He was shocked. His sister lived in Missouri. How could she be here, in Texas, standing before him? "Brother Josiah," she said, "you are too weak to go by yourself. Remain here and friends will come to take care of you." He begged his sister to stay, but she left, walking away toward Hornsby's. Wilbarger didn't understand what he'd seen. He was unsettled by the sight of his sister but also encouraged. Her words gave him the strength he needed to hope for rescue.

Meanwhile, Haynie and Standifer had made it safely back to Hornsby's Bend and told everyone there of the attack. They planned to wait a couple of days before returning to bury their friends' bodies. They wanted to make sure the coast was clear.

But that night, Rueben Hornsby's wife, Sarah, had a dream in which she saw Wilbarger wounded and scalped and without any clothes sitting by a tree. She woke in a panic, telling her husband that Josiah was alive and they needed to rescue him. Rueben tried to calm his wife, saying it was only a nightmare brought on by the disturbing story they'd told her. He coaxed her back to sleep, but the dream came again, even more real than before. This time, Sarah would not take no for an answer. She woke the men before dawn, hurried them through breakfast, and sent them on their way with sheets to wrap around Wilbarger's wounded and broken body.

When the men found Wilbarger beneath his oak tree, he was so covered in blood that at first they did not recognize him. But Wilbarger waved his arms, shouting, "It's me! It's

Wilbarger!" The search party then buried the dead. Then they wrapped Wilbarger in a sheet and took him back to Hornsby's Bend, where he rested for a few days before returning to his own home.

During the weeks of his recovery, Wilbarger made plans to contact his family in Missouri. He intended to write to them when he healed to tell his sister of his mysterious vision of her. But before he got around to it, he received a letter with distressing news: his sister Margaret was dead. She had died the day before the Comanche attack. The night her spirit visited him was the first night her body spent in the grave.

Josiah Wilbarger lived more than eleven years after the attack, but the wound in his head where he had been scalped never healed. He kept it covered as well as he could, wearing hats and scarves and even a small metal plate that he made to fit over the hole. Over time, though, disease and infection weakened his skull until his brain was exposed. When Wilbarger bumped his head on a door frame, his condition quickly worsened. He eventually died of complications from the wound.

The story of Wilbarger's incredible survival, Sarah Hornsby's prophetic dream, and Margaret Clifton's ghostly message of hope has been told for almost two hundred years now. It is considered one of the oldest ghost stories in Central Texas history.

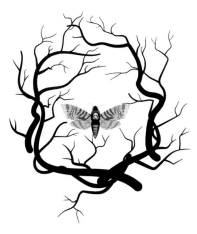

CHAPTER 3

Old Souls

At 3710 Cedar Street in central Austin sits a tan and brown building made of stone and wood that probably wouldn't grab your attention if you were walking past. But if you knew some of the things that went on inside over the years, you might take a second look.

Today, the structure on Cedar Street houses Austin Groups for the Elderly, or AGE, and the people who work there say it's haunted.

Reports of strange sounds, machinery that turns on and off by itself, and sightings of actual ghosts abound on this otherwise quiet street.

When the AGE building first opened its doors in 1908, it was the Confederate Women's Home, a facility built to house the wives and widows of Confederate soldiers. During the American Civil War, Texas sided with the Confederacy, and many women did what they could to support the Confederate soldiers. When the Union won the war in 1865, the US government provided income to the Union soldiers and their families, but the Confederate soldiers received nothing. As these soldiers grew old, many could not care for themselves. They were disabled or poor and needed help. An organization of women called the United Daughters of the Confederacy, or UDC, came to their aid. They raised money for the construction of the Confederate Men's Home in 1886.

Twenty years later, when the wives and widows of the Confederate soldiers also needed care, the UDC once again came through, opening the Confederate Women's Home on Cedar Street on June 3, 1908.

The Confederate Women's Home was much like a modern-day nursing home or assisted living facility. The women who lived there had to be at least sixty years old and prove they had participated in the Confederate war effort. Some residents were unhappy with their situation. They complained about the food or were grumpy with the staff about the care they were being given. Others were in poor health and only lived on Cedar Street a short time before passing away. However, many of the women loved living there. They spent their days knitting, quilting, or entertaining visitors.

They got along well with the staff and attended church in the parlor on Sundays. To these women, the Confederate Women's Home was truly *home*. Some of them lived in the building for thirty years.

It's understandable that some of these women would want to stick around even after their time on Earth was up, and there's evidence that a few of them may have.

One AGE staff member named Tammy was working late in her office one night when she heard a group of women talking and laughing outside her office door. The sound concerned Tammy because she'd thought she was alone, so she went to investigate. When Tammy opened the door, no one was there, and the noise abruptly stopped. But when she closed the door and returned to her desk, the chatter and laughter started up again.

Maybe the lively laughter and conversation that Tammy heard outside her office door was the happy chatter of past residents keeping up their social life in the afterlife. But not all of the eerie experiences in the current AGE building seem connected to the Confederate

Women's Home. Some seem to stem from the building's other uses.

Eventually, the number of residents at the Confederate Women's Home began to decline, and the building started to look shabby and worn down. In 1963, the last three women on the property were moved to private nursing homes, and the Confederate Women's Home closed its doors for good. The structure remained abandoned for several years until it found a new purpose.

In the 1960s, the United States suffered through an epidemic of rubella, a contagious disease that causes birth defects in the babies of infected mothers. Today, we have a vaccine to prevent this terrible disease, but in the late 1960s, we had no vaccine. Sadly, there were approximately twenty thousand children born in the United States with physical and mental disabilities such as blindness, deafness, heart defects, and other ailments due to this awful illness.

In 1972, the Confederate Women's Home was restored and remodeled for the children in the Austin area affected by the rubella epidemic. For ten years, children with disabilities stayed there. They learned life skills, received physical therapy, and played. And according to some, it's possible that some of those children are still there playing today.

A few years ago, an AGE employee named Sandy noticed the office copy machine kept

getting turned off early. No one admitted to switching off the machine, but it kept happening. It was a nuisance, because once the machine was turned off, it took a while to power up again. Sandy began to wonder if there was a timer on the machine that had been programmed incorrectly, so she called a technician. He told her there was no timer, just the large plastic switch that flipped from ON to OFF. One afternoon after that, Sandy was making copies when she turned her back to the machine for a moment. She heard a loud *CLICK*, and when she whirled around, the switch was in the OFF position. No one else was in the room. That's when Sandy knew there was more than a technological glitch at play.

Playing with a copy machine doesn't sound like something an elderly woman from the early 1900s would do, but it does sound like the action of a curious child.

The presence of ghost children could also account for the problems at the daycare. For a short time, AGE had a daycare in its building. No matter how much the staff tidied up in the evenings, the next morning they often found toys scattered around as if unseen children had played with them during the night.

Can you imagine how it would feel to be alone at work and hear the sound of a child screaming in terror? That's what happened to one AGE employee. The sound was faint but persistent and seemed to come from every direction at once, as if escaping out from the walls themselves.

Another AGE employee named Celia even thinks a playful ghost followed her home from work one day. When she drove away after leaving the office, her passenger side window started going up and down all on its own. Celia never had any problems with the window before, but no matter how many times she tried to close it, the window kept opening again. This went on so long that she took the car to a mechanic, but he found nothing wrong. Then the car's doors started locking and unlocking by themselves! At this point, Celia had an idea. She drove to AGE, parked her car, and told whoever might be in it that they couldn't come home with her and had to go back inside. She didn't have any more problems after that.

The property at 3710 Cedar Street has been the home to Austin Groups for the Elderly (AGE) since 1986, but it's clear that the building is still home to many more old souls, and some of them aren't shy about showing themselves. One AGE employee once saw a woman wearing a white suit, gloves, and a hat walk out of a storage closet on the property. She followed the oddly dressed woman to a crowded break room. The woman in white walked into the room and then vanished. A lady seated at one of the tables shivered and remarked that she just felt a sudden chill. The employee told her, "I just saw a ghost walk through."

If you decide to visit the guests at AGE, keep your eyes open. You may just see a vision of the past.

The Mysteries of Mount Bonnell

It's a warm spring evening. The sun is going down, and you're standing atop Mount Bonnell, the highest natural peak in Austin. You feel a slight ache in your legs from climbing the 102 stone steps to the top, but the pain quickly subsides as you take in the view. The orange-gold of the setting sun reflects on the waters of Lake Austin, sitting 780 feet below. The beautiful scenery and breathtaking views make it easy to understand why people think Mount Bonnell is romantic. Some couples have even chosen this West Austin landmark to say "I do." But the limestone cliffs and sharp precipices also conjure dangerous images, and legends about this picturesque place have caused some to nickname it "Lover's Leap." The most famous Mount Bonnell story is about a girl named Antonia, and it's as tragic as the tale of Romeo and Juliet.

Antonia was a young woman who came to Texas with the first Spanish explorers more than three hundred years ago. The settlers were building a mission near the present-day city of San Antonio when Antonia's beauty caught the eye of a Comanche chief. Captivated by the young maiden, the chief led a band of warriors to raid the Spanish settlement. They captured the girl and whisked her away from her family, riding north with her to their camp on the Colorado River in present-day Austin.

Antonia's parents were grief-stricken over the kidnapping of their lovely daughter, but her fiancé, Don Leal Navarro Rodriguez, refused to believe his love was lost forever. Don Leal jumped on his horse and bravely rode after her abductors. He rescued his darling Antonia, and they fled together. However, their escape was short-lived.

The Comanche warriors pursued the young couple and caught up with them at the top of Mount Bonnell, where a fatal fight took place. Determined to prevent his love from being kidnapped a second time, Don Leal fought courageously and managed to kill the Comanche chief. But during the battle, Don Leal's body was pierced by fifty arrows, and he died. Overcome with sorrow, Antonia kissed her fiancé one last time and then jumped off the rocky cliff to her own tragic death.

There is one legend of tragic love at Mount Bonnell that doesn't end in death, however: the tale of Big Foot Wallace. William A.A. "Big Foot" Wallace was a famous Texas Ranger who made a name for himself fighting for the Republic of Texas. As the legend goes, when Big Foot was in his seventies, he fell in love with a young Austin girl who did not return his affection. (This was not surprising considering the huge age difference between them.) However, Big Foot continued to woo the girl. His attempts to win her over were further thwarted when he became sick.

This was during the 1880s, when people used to take mercury to cure illnesses. They didn't know at the time about mercury poisoning and how terrible the side effects could be. Big Foot took mercury for his sickness, and it worked—sort of. He got better, but all of his hair fell out.

When the stubborn man tried *again* to get the young woman to be his wife, she told him she wouldn't marry him because he was bald. That didn't stop Big Foot Wallace. More determined than ever, he got a pot of bear grease, an herbal remedy that was supposed to make hair grow. But bear grease, which is a cream made mostly of bear fat, smells terrible, so Big Foot camped out in a cave on the cliffs of Mount Bonnell to spare others the odor.

For a month, he stayed in that cave, rubbing bear grease on his head day and night, and eventually his hair began to grow! Whether it was the bear grease or simply the passage of time that worked the magic is anyone's guess.

Cured of his baldness, Big Foot Wallace came down from Mount Bonnell to propose to his love one more time, only to find that while he was away, she had married another man. Broken-hearted, Big Foot spent the rest of his days alone. Although, he was never without his two favorite possessions: his rifle and his bowie knife, which he nicknamed "Sweetlips" and "Butch," respectively.

Such depressing and dramatic events are bound to leave their mark on a place. Maybe that's why strange mists and hazy apparitions are sometimes seen at dusk on Mount Bonnell. Visitors have reported ghostly visions and odd foggy shapes that disappear when they try to get a closer look. Could the spirits of the broken-hearted still be hovering over this scenic cliff centuries after their deaths? Maybe you should take a trip to Mount Bonnell just after sunset and see for yourself. Just be careful not to join them.

CHAPTER 5

The Ghost Wagon
of Westlake

Not all ghosts are floating specters or wispy apparitions. A ghost can be a shiver down your spine or a chilly breeze on a hot summer day. A ghost can even be a *sound*. If you spend the night on Eanes Creek in West Lake Hills, a hilly suburb of Austin known locally as "Westlake," you might just hear the spooky sound of a ghost wagon carrying the memories of its long-dead owner.

In 1991, during an investigation of illegal hunting, the Westlake police discovered an unmarked, sunken grave in the woods. They dug up the grave and found the skeleton of a man who had died over a hundred years before. Curious about the identity of this poor soul, they contacted Bruce Marshall, heir to the property that once belonged to the Eanes family.

Bruce told the police an old story he'd heard ever since he was a child, that had been passed down through his family, about a traveler murdered by bandits and left for dead on a nearby road in the late 1800s.

The story, pieced together from evidence and speculation, told of a man in a horse-drawn wagon traveling to Austin from the hill country west of town to sell his hay and purchase supplies for his farm.

He meandered along Eanes Creek until he came to the Lower Colorado River, then forded the water at a shallow point near Shoal Creek. Once in Austin, the man sold his hay, did his shopping, and had a meal on Congress Avenue before heading back home with his wagon loaded with goods.

The traveler was retracing his route when he noticed a large rock blocking the path. The road at that point was narrow, threading between Eanes Creek and a sloping hill, and it was impossible to pass without moving the small boulder, which the man was certain had not been there that morning.

The placement of the rock was suspicious, and the man undoubtedly suspected foul play. But there was no way to get around the obstacle without moving it, so he dismounted from his wagon to shove the stone aside. That's when the bandits struck. The man tried to defend himself, but he was no match for the band of thieves hiding behind the hill. He died with a bullet in his chest while the robbers made off with his money and goods.

From their home nearby, the Eanes family heard the gunshot. When they went to investigate, they found the murdered man, saw the large rock and bandits' footprints and wagon tracks, and put together what had happened. Unfortunately, they had no way of knowing who the dead man was, so they said a prayer for his soul and buried him in an unmarked grave on their property.

Over time, the tale was told, but the grave was forgotten. Eventually, the land grew up around it, and its location disappeared.

But the story doesn't end there.

In 1966, a group of parapsychologists (people who study psychic phenomena and paranormal activity) came to the

Eanes-Marshall Ranch House. They held a séance and tried to contact ghosts using automatic writing, which is where a person in contact with a spirit goes into a trance and subconsciously writes what the spirit communicates to them.

According to witnesses, there were several ghosts present that night, and one of them was a man who claimed he'd been murdered by three men after he'd gotten off his wagon to remove a stone from the road. As best as they could tell, the man identified himself as "Burns." A reporter who was at the séance was intrigued and went searching through old newspaper articles in the Austin History Center. He found a mention of a man named Barnes who had reportedly been robbed and murdered on his way back from selling hay in Austin in 1871. The only detail that didn't fit with the Eanes family's story was the location.

The article said the man had been killed seven miles *north* of the city, whereas the man buried on the Eanes property was seven miles *southwest* of the city.

Was the location in the article simply a typo? Was the man buried in the unmarked grave really this "Barnes" fellow? And, if so, had his restless spirit actually communicated with the psychic?

Regardless of the exact details of the murder, this much is true: something spooky is happening near the old Eanes property. For decades, young Austinites have camped out on Eanes Creek waiting to hear the "ghost wagon." Those who have witnessed the eerie phenomenon say you know when it's about to happen because all other sounds stop at once. The barking dogs, the birds, even the crickets hush. Then, out of the darkness, comes the gallop of hooves, the creak of wood and leather, and the rumble of wheels growing louder and louder on its ghostly ride.

Many have heard the phantom wagon, but no one has ever seen it. In fact, most were too terrified to stick around long enough to try. When a man named Joel Quintanella shared his experience hearing the ghost wagon, Bruce Marshall asked him, "What happened when it got to you?" But Joel just shook his head and admitted that, by then, he and his friends were halfway home.

What would have happened if Joel and his friends had been brave enough to wait for the ghost wagon to appear? Who—or *what*—would they have seen driving those horses?

Swen Beryman: Settler, Store Owner... Specter?

Imagine being a pioneer in the 1800s. Imagine leaving everything you know, boarding a ship, and sailing to a whole new country. Imagine doing this alone when you're only sixteen years old. Such was the case with Swen Beryman.

Swen's original last name was Bergman, but when he arrived in Galveston harbor from

Ekjo, Sweden, in 1852, immigration officials misspelled his name. From then on, he was Swen Beryman. Teenage Swen had no idea what to expect when he arrived in Texas. The state was still very much frontier land at that time. But Swen embodied the pioneer spirit. He was energetic, determined, and strong, and he worked any job that was available, learning various trades along the way. In his first ten years in Texas, Swen worked as a farm hand and a cowboy, was a blacksmith's apprentice, and drove a freight wagon.

Eventually, Swen saved enough money to buy land, cattle, and horses of his own. In 1863, he wrote to his girlfriend, a Swedish housemaid named Johanna in New York City, and she made the long, difficult journey to Texas by stagecoach. The young couple got married and settled west of Austin near present-day Johnson City.

This was during the American Civil War, and Swen and Johanna supported the Union, not the Confederacy, so there were conflicts between the young immigrants and their neighbors. Despite these challenges, the Berymans made it through the war, and their small farm was successful for fifteen years until disaster struck.

In November 1878, Swen and three companions went riding along the Devil's Backbone toward two tall peaks known back then as Long Man Mountain and Long Woman Mountain. The Devil's Backbone is a winding, hilly, limestone ridge that runs through the hill country outside of Austin. The ridge is a great place to take a drive, especially in spring when the bluebonnets are blooming. There are many scenic views along its curves. However, today this stretch of road is also considered one of the most haunted in Texas.

Long before European settlers like Swen and his wife settled in the Texas Hill Country, Native American tribes inhabited the land, and they used areas of natural beauty, such as the Devil's Backbone, as sacred religious sites. In 1878, signs of the ancient shrines could still be seen on the summits of Long Man and Long Woman Mountains, and there was already a lot of fear and superstition about the area where Swen and his group rode.

In the late afternoon, something eerie began to happen. First, the sky turned black. Then the temperature started to drop—fast. As the small party approached the trail leading to Long Woman Mountain, a frigid wind blew in, lightning lit up the sky, and they felt cold, hard pellets of hail hitting them. It was if a storm had settled just above the men. The horses began to get nervous, and everyone in the group grew fearful, except Swen. Unafraid,

Swen laughed at his friends for wanting to stop. He continued up the steep trail alone, bravely enduring the thunder and rain and dropping temperatures while the rest of the men turned back. But eventually, the storm became too much even for Swen. He dismounted from his horse and tried to find shelter among the rocks and brush along the trail.

The other men made it back to the campsite and bedded down for the night, shaking their heads at their stubborn friend. When they awoke the next morning, the storm was over, but Swen still wasn't back. They became worried and went to look for him. When they found their lost friend, he was in bad shape. Swen had not found adequate shelter, and the temperature had dropped so low during the night that his legs were frozen with frostbite. They carried him straight to the doctor, but it was too late to save his legs. Both had to be amputated.

Was this just a terrible case of bad luck? Or was something more sinister at play? Did spirits at the Devil's Backbone, angry at Swen's intrusion on their territory, create the storm that took his legs?

Swen was lucky to survive the surgery; many people did not in those days. But he was strong, and after he recovered, he learned to walk on wooden legs. However, he no longer had the ability to work a ranch, so Swen sold his home and moved his family to Oatmanville, the area of Austin that today is known as Oak Hill. There, he purchased a general store.

As manager of the store, Swen didn't let his disability get in the way of his job, and once he even prevented an outlaw from robbing him. In 1880, Brack Hendricks was on the run when he stopped into Swen's store for some tobacco and other supplies he might need while hiding out from the law. When he saw the owner of the store was an amputee, he simply helped himself to the items he wanted,

stuffing them into his pockets, ignoring Swen, even when Swen yelled at him to stop. He obviously thought a man with no legs couldn't do anything to him.

He was wrong. Swen threw a can of powdered detergent into Hendricks's eyes, blinding him. Then he hopped up onto the counter, grabbed the thief's gun from its holster while he was wiping at his eyes, removed the bullets, and hit Hendricks in the forehead with the gun. The criminal fell to the floor, stunned and choking on the stolen tobacco he'd stuffed in his mouth. Just then, the sheriff's deputy and a Texas Ranger arrived. They had seen Hendricks's stolen horse outside. They thanked Swen for catching their man and offered him reward money, but he refused.

Although Swen Beryman is long gone, the narrow, two-story stone building that housed his store in Oak Hill is still standing today.

Over the years, it served various purposes, but most Austinites know it as the location of the Austin Pizza Garden, a beloved restaurant that operated from 1994 to 2021. During the twenty-seven years the pizza place was open, more than a few strange things occurred there.

One time, the owner of the Austin Pizza Garden was preparing to leave for the night. He was the last person there. He'd stayed late to bake a pizza to take home to his family. He took the pizza out of the oven, cut it into slices, then turned away to get a box. When he turned back around, the pizza was whole again—crust, toppings, everything. But the pizza cutter the man had used was still in his hand, and it still had the melted cheese and sauce stuck to its blade.

Another creepy phenomenon was the sound of the phantom footsteps. They walked the upstairs party room on several occasions. Staff and customers in the downstairs dining room would hear them when the upstairs room was unoccupied. And sometimes, visitors attending an event in the party room itself would hear footsteps walking by, even when everyone in the room was seated. Could this be the ghost of Swen still patrolling his old store on his wooden legs?

If Swen is haunting his old building, he isn't alone. Several staff members reported seeing an old woman on the second floor near the stairwell, and she didn't seem happy with their presence. She never spoke, but she would glare at them frighteningly before disappearing. One time, an elderly woman visited the Austin Pizza Garden and asked if she could take a look around, because she had lived in the building years before it was a pizza restaurant. She wanted to see her old home one more time. The staff allowed her to walk around, and when they led her up the stairs to the second floor, she said, "Oh, this is where I used to see that mean old ghost woman!"

We may never know exactly who is haunting the old stone building at 6266 West Highway 290, but whoever it is, they don't seem to be leaving anytime soon.

The Driskill Hotel

CHAPTER 7

The Driskill Hotel

In the late 1800s, several Native American tribes occupied Central Texas, including the Comanche, Apache, Tonkawa, and Kiowa. Each tribe had its own customs and way of life, but one thing they had in common was their spirituality.

If you were a young male in the Comanche or Kiowa tribes, around the age of twelve, you would be sent on a quest to find your spirit guide. Once you found your guide, you would listen to it, allowing it to direct your decisions in life. However, if you disobeyed your spirit or refused to honor it, the spirit could become evil and turn on you.

The Comanche believed in life after death and were not afraid of ghosts. The Apache, on the other hand, were very scared of the dead. When someone in the Apache tribe died, they avoided the location of the death and buried the body as quickly as possible. When the burial was over, they left the gravesite by a different path, trying to confuse the ghost and keep it from following them.

The Tonkawa forbid anyone from speaking  the name of a dead person, for fear their name could call their spirit back. In their religion, a woman's soul went straight to a new home after death, but the soul of a man hung around, taking care of unfinished business and trying to communicate with the living. Ghosts were not welcome in the Tonkawa tribe. They believed if a soul inhabited a person's home, that person would soon die.

One commonality between the tribes was their belief in the sacred power of water. Places where clean water flowed from the earth in natural springs were treasured by the Native Americans, especially in the dry climate of Central Texas. But they didn't just appreciate the water for its life-giving benefits—they also believed the springs housed spirits.

One water source that the tribes frequently visited and believed to be a spiritual site was an artesian well in what is now downtown Austin. An artesian well is a well formed from an underground water source called an aquifer. Unlike regular wells, which use pumps to bring the water to the surface, an artesian well uses the natural pressure of the aquifer to extract water. The artesian well where the Native Americans drew water and communed with spirits was located at the corner of Sixth and Brazos Streets, which is now the home of the historic Driskill Hotel.

Colonel Jesse Driskill was a businessman who had made a lot of money rounding up the wild Texas longhorns and herding them north to be sold. In 1885, after making a profit in the cattle trade, Driskill turned his sights on Austin. The city was developing rapidly in 1885. The University of Texas had just finished its second year educating young Texans, and the current capitol was being built on Congress Avenue. Driskill's goal was to turn Sixth Street, which runs perpendicular to Congress, into a classy area, worthy of the tourists and university families that would be flocking to the city. The best way to spruce things up, he decided, was with a grand hotel.

It was no coincidence that Colonel Driskill built his hotel on the site of the artesian well. He knew the value of a dependable water source, so when he started construction on his building on July 4, 1885, he chose the location strategically.

The Driskill opened in 1886 and was just as grand as its owner had dreamed. The four-story hotel offered everything its refined guests could ask for: dining rooms, bridal apartments, a barbershop, and much more. After only two weeks of operation, the hotel hosted its first inaugural ball for Governor Sul Ross.

This seemed like a promising start for Austin's fine hotel, but trouble was on the way. The winter of 1886–1887 was unusually harsh and put many cattle barons out of business. This included

Colonel Driskill. After only six months, he was forced to close his grand hotel.

However, the Driskill did not stay closed. It opened again in 1888, and over the next eighty years, the hotel was bought and sold more than a dozen times, undergoing new ownership, renovations, and hard times. But it never lost its glory, and it never lost its name. In 1966, the Driskill became a historical site, saving it from being replaced by a parking garage and earning it a permanent place in downtown Austin.

Over the years, the Driskill has hosted inaugural balls, graduations, and weddings. In 1931, famous jazz musician Louis Armstrong played at the Driskill, and in 1934, President Lyndon B. Johnson met his wife, Lady Bird, at the hotel. President Bill Clinton stayed at the hotel in 1999, and actor Bill Murray recited a poem from its front steps in 2018. The historic Austin hotel has collected its share of memories over the years, along with a few ghost stories.

Rumors of hauntings at the Driskill have been floating around for decades. There is a legend of a little girl who died from falling down the hotel's grand staircase. Some say you can still hear her giggling. Other witnesses say some of the people in the paintings stare back at the living, and elevators will sometimes take guests to their correct floor even if they haven't pushed a button.

In 1999, two women were staying in the Driskill while attending a conference in Austin. They had heard stories that the fourth floor was haunted, and thrilled by the idea of seeing a ghost, they asked for a room there. Unfortunately, the clerk told them that floor was undergoing construction and was closed. Disappointed, the women accepted a different room. However, on their last night in the hotel, curiosity got the best of them. Around 2:00 in the morning, they went for a walk on the fourth floor, just to look around.

The clerk had told the truth. Ladders, tools, and building materials lined the hallway. But as the ladies turned to leave, they saw a woman walking down the hall carrying an armful of shopping bags. They were startled. Where had she been shopping in the middle of the night? And why was she on the closed fourth floor?

When the mysterious woman stopped in front of the door to a room at the end of the hallway, one of the guests called out, "Doesn't it bother you to stay on this floor while all the renovations are going on?"

Without turning, she replied, "No. It doesn't bother me at all."

At that moment, the two women felt a shiver go through them. They both had the feeling they were intruding and suddenly wanted to get away as quickly as possible. They hurried back to their own room.

The next morning when they checked out, the guests told the clerk about the woman they'd seen and asked why she had been given a room on the fourth floor while they had been denied. The clerk repeated that the fourth floor was closed, and no one was staying there. But the women insisted, describing what they'd seen the night before. Finally, the clerk decided to prove it. He took the guests up to the fourth floor and showed them the room they'd seen the mysterious lady enter. It was empty. The bare mattress leaned against the wall, and a brand-new toilet, waiting to be installed, sat in the middle of the room. It was a construction site, nothing more.

Although they didn't know it at the time, these shocked Driskill guests had just met the "Suicide Bride."

In the early 1980s, a young woman from Houston checked into the Driskill after her fiancé called off their wedding. Soon after arriving, she left the hotel and went on a shopping spree where she spent over $40,000 of her ex-fiancé's money. She came back to the Driskill carrying armloads of shopping bags, went to her room, and locked the door behind her. A housekeeper who noticed the woman's odd behavior called her room to see if she needed anything. The guest simply said, "Thank you, but there's nothing you can do."

More than a day later, when the woman still had not emerged and would not answer her phone or door, the housekeeper alerted the hotel manager, who called security. When they broke open the double-locked door and entered the hotel room, tragedy awaited them. The broken-hearted woman was dead. She had shot herself in the bathroom, using a pillow to muffle the sound of the gun.

The awful sight that met the housekeeper that morning still haunts her today. She was so affected by the sad discovery of the lifeless body that she scratched a small cross into the windowpane of the room on the fourth floor where the young woman died.

The ghost that the women saw on the fourth floor in 1999 was almost certainly the spirit of the Suicide Bride, but what could account for the other spooky sounds and creepy feelings that abound at the Driskill? Perhaps more of the hotel's guests have decided to "extend their stay" in this historic landmark. Or maybe the ghosts go back even further than that. Maybe the Native Americans were right, and the waters that have flowed beneath the corner of Sixth and Brazos Streets have always been alive with spirits.

Unusual
Undertakings

Have you ever wondered why people traditionally wear black to funerals? Or why the coffin is carried feet first to the gravesite? These customs were originally intended to protect the living from accidentally getting caught up in the deceased person's journey to the grave. The corpse was carried feet first so the lingering spirit did not catch the eye of a living person and lure them to follow.

Mourners wore black to the memorial service in order to draw less attention to themselves; they didn't want to be seen by the dead. It was also considered bad luck to interrupt a funeral procession, because it might interfere with the soul's journey to the afterlife.

But not all funeral procedures were based on fantastical beliefs. Most were performed out of necessity to keep the body preserved for viewing before the burial. In the 1800s, most undertakers were cabinetmakers or furniture-makers who extended their business to include coffins and then began to "undertake" the responsibilities of assisting a family who had experienced a death. It was the undertaker's job to measure the body for the coffin, build the coffin, prepare the body for the funeral, transport the coffin to the cemetery, and bury it or oversee the burial.

In the late 1800s, if a family in Austin lost a loved one, they would most likely be doing business with Joseph Hannig.

Hannig was the fifth and final husband of Susanna Wilkerson, who was famous for being one of the few survivors of the Battle of the Alamo. Although her first husband, Lieutenant Almaron Dickinson, perished in that fateful fight in 1836, Susanna and her baby girl escaped with their lives. After a series of unsuccessful marriages and hardships, Susanna married Joseph Hannig. They moved to Austin in the early 1870s, and Hannig set up shop at 204 East Sixth Street.

Funerals were not the same back then as they are today. The biggest difference is they usually took place in the deceased person's home, in the front parlor or in the bedroom. The coffin was transported to the house in the "dead wagon," which was a wagon built specially to carry coffins and corpses. Some were fancy and some were plain, but the most important thing was that they were well-ventilated.

When the dead wagon left Hannig's business on Sixth Street, people watched and children followed, all curious to see where it was going and to learn who had died.

At the house of the deceased, the undertaker either used a cooling board or an embalming kit to prepare the body for viewing. A cooling board was a folding table with holes drilled in it. A block of ice was placed underneath the table, and the body was placed on top. The ice and ventilation allowed air to circulate, keeping the corpse cool.

A cooling board was the usual method of preserving a body for an in-home funeral until after the American Civil War, when traveling salesmen began selling embalming kits in the South. Embalming is a way of using chemicals to preserve a body after death, and the kits provided undertakers with everything they needed to perform the procedure. Soon, this more modern method became the norm.

Some of these tasks may seem morbid or unpleasant, but they were all done as a way to show respect and dignity to the deceased person and the loved ones left behind. By preserving the body in this way, undertakers gave family and friends a chance to say goodbye.

After the funeral, Hannig's dead wagon would return to take the coffin to Oakwood Cemetery. Oakwood is Austin's oldest graveyard. It was founded in 1839 on the highest hill in east Austin. The cemetery covers more than forty acres and is the final resting place of many of Austin's elite, including Joseph Hannig and his wife, Susanna.

The Hannig Building still exists. Built in 1876 in the Renaissance Revival style, the sturdy but decorative structure stands out on present-day Sixth Street. It has changed ownership and purpose over the years, but the ornate windows and beautiful architecture still remain. In 2000, the building became the home of BD Riley's Irish Pub, and rumors of ghosts started to spread. What made people think the place was haunted? Well, there are plenty of stories—take your pick!

One unsettling occurrence was the movement of objects by unseen hands. Items on desks in the upstairs offices frequently rearranged themselves during the night. Then there was the smell: in the back rooms of the pub's first floor, a strong floral scent often wafted through the air from no apparent source. Finally, there was an unshakable feeling people sometimes got. One of BD Riley's managers often had the sense of being watched when he arrived at the pub to open. At times, he thought he saw out of the corner of his eye a man sitting at the bar. But if he turned his head for a better look, the image would disappear.

It's natural to think the Hannig Building's ghosts would originate from the structure's days as an undertaking business. But remember, back then funerals took place in homes. The deceased were never housed at 204 East Sixth Street. So who was haunting BD Riley's?

One theory is that the ghosts arrived along with the decor and furniture brought over from Ireland for the pub. Spirits can sometimes attach to objects. Maybe the smells and apparitions belonged to souls lonesome for their home country. Or maybe they came from one of the building's other inhabitants over

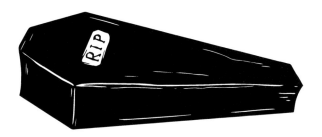

the years. Then again, perhaps the hauntings did originate from Hannig's undertaking business. Maybe there was some truth to those superstitions about funeral procedures after all. Did the old Austin undertaker catch the eye of a spirit on its way to the grave? Did a lost soul follow him home and decide to stay in the Sixth Street building?

BD Riley's closed in 2020, and as of the writing of this book, the historic building is still waiting for a new owner. But no one knows whether or not the ghosts have left the premises, so hopefully whoever moves in is open to some company.

Texas State Capitol

The Governing Ghosts of the Texas Capitol

At 1100 Congress Avenue in downtown Austin stands the Texas Capitol, a building that embodies the beauty and grandeur of the great state it represents. Made from pink granite and limestone, with elegant staircases, ornate columns, and interesting details at every turn—even the door hinges are decorative— the capitol is a point of pride for the people of

Texas. Its dome reaches 302 feet, or the length of a football field, up into the sky, making it one of the largest capitol buildings in the country.

When guests visit this impressive house of government, they sometimes encounter more than they expect. Mysterious mists and unexplained lights have been reported on the capitol grounds for years, and some of the officials wandering the halls are not of this world. Who are the ghosts who roam the Texas Capitol? A look at the building's past provides some theories.

The current capitol in Austin was not the first to exist in its present location. The original building was erected in 1853, but it burned to the ground on November 9, 1881. The following year, construction on the current capitol began.

After the American Civil War ended, criminal

activity increased in the Southern states. There were so many people behind bars the prisons were overcrowded. Texas did not have the money or the space to house all of the inmates. The capitol was under construction at this time, and a lot of manpower was needed to create such a large, ornate structure. The contractors came up with a way to solve both problems: they would use convicts to build the capitol.

Charles B. Farwell, John Villiers Farwell, and Abner Taylor, collectively known as the Capitol Syndicate, contracted thousands of inmates to work for them. More than half of the convicts were black, even though African Americans only made up 25 percent of the population at the time. The Capitol Syndicate paid the state 65¢ a day for each prisoner in exchange for giving them food, clothing, and a place to sleep. But there were few regulations back then, and no one had the convicts' well-being in mind. They were severely mistreated. Some refer to the convict leasing program as "slavery by another name."

Furthermore, the work itself was dangerous. Limestone from the quarry in Oatmanville (present-day Oak Hill) was collected to make the inside walls of the capitol, while red granite from Granite Mountain in Burnet County was used for the exterior of the building. The cutting, shaping, and hauling of all this heavy stone was done by the prisoners. During the six years of construction, a total of fifteen thousand railroad cars of stone rolled to Austin just for the outer walls alone. Inmates also did the ironwork for the dome and much of the decorative work for the interior.

Although the exact numbers are unclear, it is rumored that at least a few men died during the capitol construction, either from accidents or poor working conditions, but their names have been lost to history. The inmates' lives held little value to those in charge, and their deaths went unrecognized.

The blood those men shed for the construction of the capitol didn't leave a mark on the official record, but it may have stained the memory of the place. Some of the spirits that haunt the halls of the capitol may belong to those ill-treated convicts who died during construction. It makes sense that their souls would be restless after suffering such an unceremonious end.

Another possible source of one of the ghosts could be a man named Matt Hansen, who died in 1983 during another fire at the capitol. Hansen was a guest of Lieutenant Governor

William P. Hobby Jr. When flames engulfed the guest suite in the middle of the night, he was unable to escape and died of smoke inhalation. He was only twenty-three years old.

Although some speculate that the mysterious mists and ghostly sightings could stem from the deaths of the inmates and Matt Hansen, the most famous spirit in the Texas Capitol is definitely Colonel R.M. Love.

Colonel Love served as the state comptroller in 1903. He was sitting at his desk in the east wing at 10:00 in the morning on June 30 when a man named W.G. Hill entered Colonel Love's office and handed him a letter. Unaware that Hill was a former state employee who blamed Love for the loss of his job, the colonel took the letter and began to read. Hill's words were filled with accusations and venom as well as quotes from Shakespeare. He had written, "You have robbed the state's employees, and your incompetent administration has permitted others to rob the state." He accused Love of murdering him by taking away his livelihood and ended the letter by quoting Frederick Douglass: "For the right against the wrong. For the weak against the strong."

While Colonel Love read the letter, Hill drew a gun from his pocket and shot the man in the chest.

Several people nearby heard the shot and rushed to Colonel Love's office. Mr. Stephens, the bookkeeper, arrived in time to see Hill fire a second shot. He quickly tackled the gunman. Reverend Cowden, who had just been talking to Colonel Love before Hill's arrival, and Annie Stanfield, Love's stenographer, hurried in to find Hill and Stephens wrestling on the ground. After a tense moment of suspense, Stephens stood up, leaving the gunman on the ground in a pool of blood. He, too, had been shot in the chest.

Hill reached into his pocket and pulled out a bottle of laudanum, a powerful painkiller, but

Stephens slapped it from his hand. He would not allow Hill to ease his own death after what he had done to the comptroller.

Colonel Love stood up. "I've been shot," he said. He tried to walk but collapsed. A crowd had gathered by this time. They placed Colonel Love on a couch in his office and made him as comfortable as possible. Then they sent for his family. A little over an hour later, Love's wife, son, and sisters were at his side when he took his final breath. According to a reporter from the *Austin Statesman*, Colonel Love left this world with compassion in his heart. His last words were, "Ah, God forgive and save him who hath robbed me of my life."

The comptroller's assassination had a profound effect on the community. But, although Colonel Love had died, some argued that he was not completely gone. Shortly after the shooting, reports began of a man walking through the east wing who faded away or dissolved into mist. People who saw him speculated that it was the spirit of Colonel Love, still walking the halls outside his office. Now, over a hundred years later, people still talk of an oddly dressed man in old-fashioned clothes who nods in greeting or even says "Good day" before disappearing without a trace.

An intern at the capitol was talking on the phone with her mother in the east wing one day when a man passed her and said "Good evening." Not wanting to appear rude to an official, she ended her call quickly and turned to respond to the man, but he was gone. Later, when someone showed her a photo of the colonel, she exclaimed, "That's him! I recognize the bushy mustache!"

Unlike most ghosts, who seem to be a bit shy in front of photographers, Colonel Love has even been spotted on the capitol's security cameras. Once in a while, the footage shows a crowd of people when suddenly an oddly dressed man appears in the frame. Other times, a person will mysteriously disappear from the camera's image between one second and the next.

The Texas Capitol is a great place to visit if you're interested in government, architecture, history, or Texas culture, but it's also a good place to go for a chance to meet someone from the next world. If you see Colonel Love, be sure to tell him hello.

Last Words

It's clear that visitors to Austin have many options when it comes to sightseeing. Whether they choose to make a stop at famous buildings like the Texas Capitol and the Driskill or spend time outdoors at Mount Bonnell or Red Bud Isle, there's a chance they'll encounter evidence of the supernatural. They may be taking a stroll down Sixth Street when an unexpected shiver sneaks up their spine, or they may be wading in the waters of Lake Austin when they see an eerie glowing orb. After all, Austin's history runs deep, but some of its past refuses to stay buried. You might just run into some of it while you're here.

Carie Juettner was born on Halloween and has loved ghost stories ever since. By day, she is a middle school English teacher, but by night, she is a writer of poems and short stories and novels. Carie lives in Austin, Texas, with her husband and pets, but she loves to travel. One of her favorite things to do on vacation is visit cemeteries and learn about local lore.

Check out some of the other Spooky America titles available now!

Spooky America was adapted from the creeptastic Haunted America series for adults. Haunted America explores historical haunts in cities and regions across America. Each book chronicles both the widely known and less-familiar history behind local ghosts and other unexplained mysteries. Here's more from *Haunted Austin* author Jeanine Plumer: